SELF-IMPROVEMENT

Femi Amosun

"Self-Improvement"

Femi Amosun

Table of Contents

Chapter I.

Introduction

Are you ready to take your life to the next level? Do you want to become the best version of yourself? If so, then "Self-Improvement" is the book for you.

In this comprehensive guide, you will learn about the importance of self-improvement and how it can help you achieve your goals, overcome challenges, and live a more fulfilling life. This book covers a wide range of topics related to personal growth and development, from setting goals and improving your mindset to boosting your productivity and building strong, healthy relationships.

Chapter by chapter, you will explore techniques, strategies, and tips to help you unleash your full potential. Here's a brief overview of the topics covered in the book:

Chapter II: Setting Goals - You will learn about the importance of setting goals, how to set achievable goals, and strategies for staying motivated and on track.

Chapter III: Mindset - You will discover how your mindset affects personal growth and learn techniques for developing a growth mindset and overcoming limiting beliefs.

Chapter IV: Productivity - You will explore techniques for improving productivity and time management, strategies for prioritizing tasks and reducing distractions, and tips for maintaining focus and avoiding procrastination.

Chapter V: Communication - You will understand the importance of effective communication in personal and professional relationships, techniques for improving communication skills, and strategies for resolving conflicts and managing difficult conversations.

Chapter VI: Health and Wellness - You will discover the connection between physical and mental health, tips for developing healthy habits, and strategies for managing stress and improving overall well-being.

Chapter VII: Relationships - You will explore the importance of healthy relationships in personal and professional life, techniques for building and maintaining strong relationships, and strategies for setting healthy boundaries and managing conflicts.

Chapter VIII: Conclusion - You will recap the key topics covered in the book, offer final thoughts on the importance of self-improvement and personal growth, and provide a call to action for readers to implement the strategies and techniques discussed in the book.

By the end of **"Self-Improvement,"** you will have the tools and knowledge you need to unlock your full potential and live the life you've always dreamed of. Get ready to embark on a journey of self-discovery and personal growth.

Chapter II

Setting Goals

Is an essential part of personal growth and development. Without clear objectives and targets to aim for, it's easy to get stuck in a rut or feel directionless. In this chapter, we'll explore why setting goals is so important, techniques for setting achievable goals, and strategies for staying motivated and on track.

Explanation of why setting goals is important:

Setting goals provides a sense of purpose and direction. When you have a clear idea of what you want to achieve, you can focus your energy and efforts in the right direction. Goals also help you measure progress and celebrate milestones, boosting your confidence and motivation.

Techniques for setting achievable goals:

To set achievable goals, it's important to follow some key principles:

Make them **SMART:** Specific, Measurable, Attainable, Relevant, and Time-bound. This means setting goals that are clear, quantifiable, realistic, relevant to your values and priorities, and have a deadline.

Break them down into smaller steps: Large goals can be overwhelming, so breaking them down into smaller, more manageable tasks can help you make progress without feeling daunted.

Write them down: This helps you clarify your goals, commit to them, and track your progress.

Strategies for staying motivated and on track:

Setting goals is one thing, but staying motivated and on track is another. Here are some strategies to help you stay focused and committed to your goals:

Visualize success: Visualize yourself achieving your goal, and imagine how it will feel. This can boost your motivation and keep you on track.

Track your progress: Regularly review your progress and celebrate your achievements. This can give you a sense of accomplishment and encourage you to keep going.

Surround yourself with support: Share your goals with friends, family, or a supportive community. Having a support system can help you stay accountable, motivated, and focused on your goals.

By following these techniques and strategies, you'll be able to set achievable goals and stay motivated and on track. In the next chapter, we'll explore how your mindset affects your ability to achieve your goals and how to develop a growth mindset for success.

Chapter III

Mindset

Your mindset plays a crucial role in your personal growth and development. The way you think about yourself and your abilities can either hold you back or propel you forward. In this chapter, we'll explore how your mindset affects your personal growth, techniques for developing a growth mindset, and strategies for overcoming limiting beliefs.

How mindset affects personal growth:

Your mindset is the lens through which you see the world. If you have a fixed mindset, you believe that your abilities and traits are innate and cannot be changed. On the other hand, if you have a growth mindset, you believe that your abilities can be developed through hard work and perseverance. This belief can significantly impact your personal growth and potential.

Techniques for developing a growth mindset:

Here are some techniques for developing a growth mindset:

Embrace challenges: Instead of avoiding challenges, view them as opportunities for growth and learning. Embracing challenges can help you develop resilience and adaptability.

Learn from failure: Failure is a natural part of the learning process. Instead of giving up, use failure as an opportunity to reflect, learn, and grow.

Cultivate a passion for learning: Embrace lifelong learning by seeking out new experiences, exploring new interests, and taking on new challenges.

Strategies for overcoming limiting beliefs:

Limiting beliefs are negative thoughts or self-talk that hold you back from reaching your full potential. Here are some strategies for overcoming limiting beliefs:

Identify and challenge negative self-talk: Start by recognizing negative self-talk and questioning its validity. Ask yourself if there is evidence to support it, and challenge it with positive affirmations.

Reframe your perspective: Reframe negative experiences as opportunities for growth and learning. Focus on what you've learned or gained from the experience.

Surround yourself with positivity: Surround yourself with positive people, resources, and experiences that support your growth and development.

By developing a growth mindset and overcoming limiting beliefs, you'll be able to unlock your full potential and achieve your goals. In the next chapter, we'll explore techniques for improving productivity and time management.

Chapter IV:

Productivity

In today's fast-paced world, productivity is more important than ever. Being productive means making the most of your time, accomplishing tasks efficiently, and achieving your goals. In this chapter, we'll explore techniques for improving productivity and time management, strategies for prioritizing tasks and reducing distractions, and tips for maintaining focus and avoiding procrastination.

Techniques for improving productivity and time management:

Here are some techniques for improving productivity and time management:

Create a schedule: Use a planner or digital tool to create a schedule that outlines your daily tasks, appointments, and deadlines. Having a visual representation of your time can help you manage it more effectively.

Use the Pomodoro technique: The Pomodoro technique involves breaking work into 25-minute intervals, followed by a short break. This technique can help you stay focused and increase your productivity.

Minimize multitasking: Multitasking can actually decrease your productivity. Instead, focus on one task at a time and give it your full attention.

Strategies for prioritizing tasks and reducing distractions:

Here are some strategies for prioritizing tasks and reducing distractions:

Use the Eisenhower matrix: The Eisenhower matrix involves categorizing tasks based on their urgency and importance. This can help you prioritize tasks and focus on the most important ones.

Limit distractions: Distractions, such as social media or email notifications, can significantly reduce your productivity. Try turning off notifications or using a productivity app that blocks distractions.

Delegate tasks: Delegating tasks to others can help you free up time and focus on more important tasks.

Tips for maintaining focus and avoiding procrastination:

Here are some tips for maintaining focus and avoiding procrastination:

Break tasks into smaller steps: Breaking tasks into smaller, more manageable steps can make them less overwhelming and easier to tackle.

Reward yourself: Set up a reward system for yourself after completing tasks. This can help motivate you to stay on track and avoid procrastination.

Get enough rest: Rest and relaxation are crucial for maintaining focus and productivity. Make sure to get enough sleep and take breaks throughout the day.

By implementing these techniques and strategies, you'll be able to improve your productivity and achieve your goals more efficiently. In the next chapter, we'll explore the importance of effective communication in personal and professional relationships.

Chapter V

Communication

Effective communication is an essential aspect of personal and professional relationships. It involves exchanging ideas, thoughts, and feelings with others while listening and understanding their perspectives. Communication skills are crucial in our day-to-day lives, from expressing ourselves to negotiating with others. In this chapter, we will explore the importance of effective communication and provide techniques and strategies to improve your communication skills.

The Importance of Effective Communication

Effective communication is essential for building healthy relationships, improving teamwork, and increasing productivity. When communication is done correctly, it can create trust and respect between individuals, increase motivation, and improve problem-solving. On the other hand, poor communication can lead to misunderstandings, conflicts, and breakdowns in relationships.

Techniques for Improving Communication Skills

involve developing both verbal and nonverbal communication techniques. Verbal communication includes speaking, listening, and responding. Nonverbal communication includes body language, tone of voice, and facial expressions. In this section, we will provide techniques for improving both verbal and nonverbal communication skills.

Strategies for Resolving Conflicts and Managing Difficult Conversations

Conflicts are an inevitable part of personal and professional relationships. However, it's essential to manage conflicts effectively to avoid negative outcomes. Managing difficult conversations involves active listening, empathy, and problem-solving skills. In this section, we will provide strategies for resolving conflicts and managing difficult conversations, including techniques for active listening, reframing negative statements, and understanding different communication styles.

Chapter VI

Health & Wellness

Health and wellness are crucial aspects of personal growth and self-improvement. It involves taking care of both physical and mental health to improve overall well-being. In this chapter, we will explore the connection between physical and mental health, and provide tips for developing healthy habits, and strategies for managing stress.

The Connection Between Physical and Mental Health

Physical and mental health are interconnected. A healthy body and mind can help reduce stress, improve mood, increase energy, and enhance overall well-being. Neglecting one's physical health can lead to mental health issues such as anxiety and depression. In this section, we will explore the connection between physical and mental health and the importance of taking care of both.

Tips for Developing Healthy Habits

Is essential for maintaining good physical and mental health. It involves adopting healthy eating habits, regular exercise, getting enough sleep, and avoiding harmful substances. In this section, we will provide tips for developing healthy habits, including creating a daily routine, setting realistic goals, and tracking progress.

Strategies for Managing Stress and Improving Overall Well-being

Stress is a common issue that affects many individuals' physical and mental health. Managing stress involves adopting healthy coping mechanisms, such as relaxation techniques and regular exercise. In this section, we will provide strategies for managing stress and improving overall well-being, including mindfulness techniques, time management strategies, and setting boundaries.

By implementing the tips and strategies provided in this chapter, readers can improve their physical and mental health and enhance their overall well-being.

Chapter VII

Relationships

Healthy relationships are a key component of a happy and fulfilling life, both personally and professionally. In this chapter, we will explore the importance of building and maintaining strong relationships, as well as strategies for setting healthy boundaries and managing conflicts.

The importance of healthy relationships in personal and professional life Having positive relationships with others is essential for our well-being. Studies have shown that people with strong social connections tend to be happier and healthier than those who are isolated. Good relationships can provide emotional support, motivation, and a sense of belonging. Building strong relationships at work can also enhance teamwork, communication, and productivity.

Techniques for building and maintaining strong relationships Building strong relationships takes effort, but it is a skill that can be learned. In this section, we will explore techniques for building and maintaining strong relationships, such as active listening, empathy, and showing appreciation. We will also discuss ways to nurture existing relationships, including staying in touch and making time for quality interactions.

Strategies for setting healthy boundaries and managing conflicts In any relationship, it is important to set healthy boundaries and communicate them clearly. This can help prevent misunderstandings and conflicts down the line. In this section, we will explore strategies for setting healthy boundaries, such as being assertive and learning to say "no" when necessary. We will also discuss techniques for managing conflicts when they do arise, including active listening, empathy, and compromise.

Chapter VIII

Conclusion

In this book, we've explored various ways to improve oneself and achieve personal growth. We covered a wide range of topics including goal setting, mindset, productivity, communication, health and wellness, and relationships. By understanding these areas and developing strategies and techniques to improve them, we can achieve a better version of ourselves.

In conclusion, self-improvement is a lifelong journey that requires commitment and perseverance. It's important to continuously strive to learn, grow, and develop new skills. By implementing the techniques and strategies discussed in this book, we can overcome limiting beliefs, develop a growth mindset, and build better habits to achieve our goals.

Remember, self-improvement is a personal journey that requires individual efforts, and the journey may not always be easy. But it's a journey worth taking because it leads to a better life, improved relationships, and a more fulfilling future.

As a final thought, I want to encourage you to take action and implement the strategies and techniques discussed in this book. Don't just read this book and forget about it; take the necessary steps to apply the knowledge and transform your life. Whether you want to improve your productivity, communication skills, or relationships, start today and commit to continuous self-improvement.

First book written and published